SOMERSET MOODS

Christopher Nicholson

HALSGROVE

First published in Great Britain in 2004

Title page photograph: *Exmoor from Selworthy Green.*

British Library Cataloguing-in-Publication Data
A CIP record for this title is available from the British Library

ISBN 1 84114 386 3

HALSGROVE
Halsgrove House
Lower Moor Way
Tiverton, Devon EX16 6SS
Tel: 01884 243242
Fax: 01884 243325
email: sales@halsgrove.com
website: www.halsgrove.com

Printed and bound by Oriental Press

INTRODUCTION

Somerset – 'Land of the Summer People' is its ancient meaning. The same could be true today as Somerset continues to attract a huge influx of summer visitors. Why do they come? Mostly because of its natural beauty that they can walk, drive or cycle through. Somerset has such a diverse range of scenery that finding something of interest is not difficult for the visitor: golden beaches, rocky cliffs, wild moorland, rolling hills, and flat marshlands – Somerset has them all.

It can even provide visitors with a traditional seaside holiday at its assorted resorts. Here are the piers, harbours, beach stalls, donkeys, boat hire, cararvan sites and even full-blown holiday camps for those that seek such amenities. Then, there are its historical associations and buildings. Somerset is just one of the various places in England where King Arthur lived (and died!) and has many other religious and mythological connections dotted throughout its length. Glastonbury was a popular summer destination for travellers long before the pop festival started, and prehistoric man was living in the caves of Mendip thousands of years ago.

With such a wealth of subjects within a short driving distance, Somerset is a wonderful place for a photographer to live. Panoramic landscapes, big skies, ever-changing seascapes, historical architecture, grand houses, thatched cottages and natural history are just some of the subjects to point a camera at. And that's just what I've been doing now for over twenty-five years. I still haven't exhausted all the subjects and still find new ones every year, and every year something has changed with some of the ones I've already photographed – if only the weather or the season.

For this book I have included images taken within the boundaries of the 'old' county of Somerset (prior to 1974) – including what is now called North Somerset – but not of Bristol or Bath and its environs. If you live in Somerset, or know it well, I hope you will find something of interest as you turn these pages. If your particular favourite part of the county doesn't feature in any of the photographs I offer my apologies. It has been impossible to cover every corner or aspect of life in the county within this modest volume. I've tried to choose photographs that show the kind of places or views that both attract me and – apparently – all of those people who return to the Land of the Summer People year after year.

Chris Nicholson
January 2004

LOCATION MAP

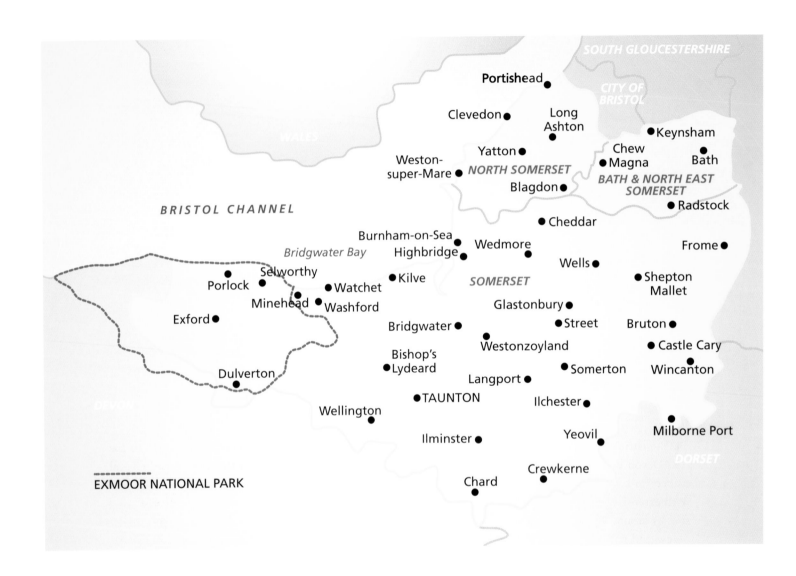

THE COAST

The entire Somerset coastline stretches along the Bristol Channel from Portishead in the north to the Devon border not far from Lynmouth. Along this 60 or so miles is some of the most varied coastal scenery to be found anywhere along the south-western peninsula. There are miles of golden sands backed with extensive sand dunes between Brean and Burnham, towering cliffs covered in native British woodland species around Porlock, and in between comes a mixture of sea-rounded pebbles, crumbling cliffs, rocky ledges and miles of mud flats. Such diversity has drawn visitors for many generations who come to walk, drive or cycle through this natural beauty. Even the alternative 'beauty' of Weston-super-Mare, Burnham-on-Sea or Minehead sometimes has its attractions.

The recently restored Victorian elegance of Clevedon Pier attracts many visitors. Beyond is the coast of Wales.

Above: *No slot machines or theatre at the end of this pier. Its restoration has been tastefully and sympathetically done to retain its Victorian appearance.*

Overleaf: *Low tide at Weston-super-Mare – a common sight – exposes acres of sand and mud flats. Beyond is the whaleback of Brean Down.*

When the sea returns, the boats moored in the harbour bob back to life in front of the Knightstone Theatre.

On the Grand Pier at Weston-super-Mare amusements, ice-creams and family fun are the order of the day.
When the tide is out hardy bathers can enjoy the delights of the tidal pool on the beach!

The Grand Pier was built in 1933 and still retains much of its art-deco styling.

*Weston is very much a 'traditional' seaside
resort, one of the attractions of which
is a donkey ride on the beach.*

Every possible item of beach paraphernalia is available from Weston's well-stocked beach stalls.

From the summit of Brean Down, exactly how far the tide recedes at low water can be seen clearly – so too can Weston's original pier on Birnbeck Island.

Looking south from Brean Down reveals the start of 5 miles of unbroken beach. On the horizon is the distinctive silhouette of Brent Knoll.

*When the red stripe on the unusual stilted lighthouse at Burnham-on-Sea is lined up with the red stripe
on the High Light behind, it indicates the safe passage into the mouth of the River Parrett.*

Above: *Late afternoon sun and scudding clouds are reflected in the pools left on Burnham beach.*

Opposite: *West of the River Parrett the coastline becomes rocky. Kilve is notable
for the huge numbers of fossilised ammonites found amongst its rocky ledges.*

Above: *At Blue Anchor Bay the wheat fields extend to the very edge of the cliffs. Across the bay lie Dunster and Minehead.*

Opposite: *Just west of Kilve is where the Quantock ridge tumbles into the sea in a series of crumbling cliffs.*

Minehead is another Victorian seaside resort with typical seafront hotels, an esplanade and shelters. As the town grew it expanded to fill up the slopes of North Hill.

Above: *Its harbour is set against a backdrop of picturesque wooded cliffs.*

West of Minehead is the huge bulk of Selworthy Beacon. The pebble ridge in Porlock Bay that was breached by winter storms can also be seen.

Porlock Weir is a particularly attractive tidal creek nestling under the wooded slopes of Exmoor and the home berth for a small number of yachts.

THE LEVELS

The Somerset 'Levels' is the name given to the thousands of acres of billard-table-flat wetlands that extend inland from the Bristol Channel coast between Bridgwater and the Mendips. They have become an internationally important area for flora and fauna because of the unique habitat they provide. In Roman times, they were mainly swamp and marshland drained by a few silty rivers that at one time were navigable inland as far as the port of Glastonbury! Since then they have been drained and turned into fertile agricultural land where cows graze and crops grow, although even today during wet winters they are frequently submerged by several feet of water. There are hardly any fences on the Levels to separate the fields of this flat landscape – this is done by the straight drainage ditches around each field known as rhynes (pronounced 'rheens'). Lining these drainage rhynes are the characteristic willow trees that have become almost a trademark of the unique Somerset Levels.

Above: *The top of Burrow Mump gives a good view of the Levels – acres of flat land, drained by miles of rhynes lined with hundreds of willow trees.*

Opposite: *As well as draining the Levels and preventing their return to marshland, the rhynes are the watery fences that keep livestock in their fields.*

Overleaf: *Some of these drainage rhynes are large enough to have 'river' status. This is the River Brue that drains South Moor near Glastonbury.*

Above: *Early morning mist collects above King's Sedgemoor between the Polden Hills and High Ham.*

Opposite: *The Levels are the home to huge numbers of swans – like these two and their cygnet heading along the Cripps River on a winter's afternoon.*

Above: *Early morning on the Levels. The winter flooding has created a perfect reflection of the willow tree in the Cripps River.*

Opposite: *Snow doesn't come very often to the Levels, but when it does its transformation of the willow trees can be magical.*

During really wet winters the rhynes can't cope and the fields themselves flood — sometimes to a depth of several feet.

This is the most valuable commodity on the Somerset Levels – peat – which is voraciously extracted and left to dry before being sold to the horticultural industry.

Left: *The two biggest rivers that drain the Levels are the Parrett (on the left) and the Tone (on the right) – and this is their confluence just beneath Burrow Mump.*

Overleaf: *A typical winter sunset across the Huntspill River.*

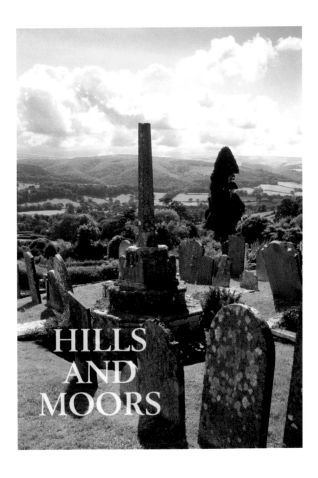

HILLS
AND
MOORS

The far west of Somerset contains some of the highest land in the south west. Only Dartmoor has higher summits than the wild moors of Exmoor. Its proximity to the coast means that as it tumbles to the sea it produces dramatic cliff scenery. Further to the north-east is the equally impressive range of hills known as Mendip – a huge limestone plateau eaten into by gorges like Cheddar and riddled with underground passages and caves that attract the potholing community. In between are less dramatic but equally beautiful ranges of hills. The Brendons and Blackdowns have rolling hills and deep valleys, while the Quantocks are a smaller version of Exmoor with herds of red deer wandering across its ridges or through its wooded combes. One of Somerset's smaller ranges of hills is the Poldens – only 300 or so feet high but rising dramatically out of the acres of flat levels to their north and south.

At 1705ft Dunkery Beacon is Somerset's highest point – a smooth rounded summit only 4 miles from the coast. This is the view of Dunkery from Selworthy.

Above: The summit is marked by a cairn bearing a plaque commemorating its hand-over to the National Trust in 1935. On a fine day the views from here are stunning.

Overleaf: This view shows Dunkery from the north-west in high summer. The road that snakes its way up from Porlock is visible on the left.

Looking directly north from Dunkery reveals the Bristol Channel and the coast and hills of Wales beyond. Lit by the sunlight is the whitewashed church at Selworthy.

To the east the views can extend as far as Bridgwater Bay, Weston-super-Mare and the Mendips.

There aren't many trees above a certain altitude on Exmoor and this is one of the few that has survived. Beyond are the rolling Brendon Hills.

The Chains ridge – close to the border of Somerset and Devon – is another of Exmoor's high points.

The Quantock Hills are a mixture of open moorland and wooded valleys or 'combes'. The myriad shades of green seen here are from the new season's leaf growth in May.

Dappled sunlight through the leaves of a beech tree light up the forest floor on the way up to the highest point of the Quantocks at Wills Neck.

Opposite: Wild ponies are a common sight on the Quantocks, particularly this group that live on Cothelstone Hill near the trees on the summit known as the Seven Sisters.

Right: Solitary ponies and their offspring are also regularly seen on the Quantocks — like this pair above Plainsfield.

The northern fringes of Somerset are dominated by the extensive ridge of the Mendip Hills. This view across the Levels near Wedmore shows the plateau to good effect.

Cheddar Gorge is Somerset's No.1 tourist attraction – and no wonder. The towering limestone cliffs
are the remnants of a collapsed cave system from prehistoric times.

Even on the top of the ridge it is possible to grow crops — as this field of barley shows.
The drystone walls are very much characteristic of the Mendip landscape.

Above: *The Polden Hills are only gentle, but are notable because they separate the two huge areas of the Somerset Levels on either side. This is looking south towards Stawell village.*

Opposite: *The walls are constructed from the carboniferous limestone of the Mendips. This view is looking south across the Somerset Levels and shows a fine crop of ragwort.*

Rare winter snow on the Polden Hills. A farm track in the village of Cossington glistens as a weak sun shines on the ice-covered walls.

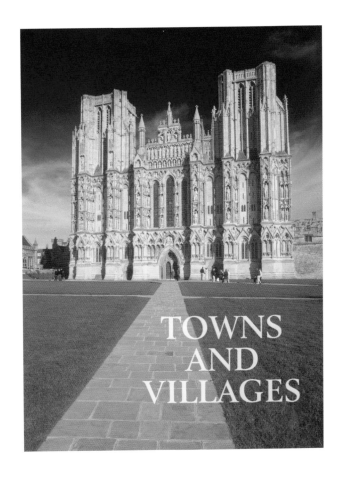

TOWNS
AND
VILLAGES

Somerset, being a rural county, has comparatively few large towns and only one city. That distinction goes to Wells – home of the county's only cathedral, although the city is actually smaller than the county town of Taunton. Apart from these two, Bridgwater, Street, Glastonbury, Wellington, Shepton Mallet, Wincanton, Weston-super-Mare and Yeovil are the main centres of population. However, the one thing that Somerset does have in abundance is villages. Most of these are working agricultural communities, but it also has the real tourist traps, complete with thatched cottages, village greens and tearooms. There are pack-horse bridges, market crosses and gift shops a-plenty in some of Somerset's prettiest villages. No wonder they are such regular favourites for the calendar publishers.

Taunton is Somerset's county town and home to St Mary Magdalene church. This has Somerset's highest church tower which was completely rebuilt in 1862.

The Castle dates from 1138 and was the focus of various activities during the Wars of the Roses and the Civil War. Today it is the home of the County Museum.

Vivary Park is the biggest open space in the town. Its intricate gates date from 1895.

Jellalabad Barracks – the former home of the Somerset Light Infantry – overlook the park and the iron fountain erected in memory of Queen Victoria.

Bridgwater's magnificent Georgian terrace on Castle Street was completed in 1730, but to be able to admire it like this — without parked cars — is a rare sight indeed.

The town was once a thriving inland port on the River Parrett. Tall ships could get as far as the bridge here and unload into the warehouses lining the quay.

The architecture of the buildings that line West Quay – with their many different influences – is one of the best features of the town.

Opposite: *It is the sheer beauty of the stonework on the west front of Wells Cathedral that draws thousands of visitors every year. It is best viewed with a setting sun in late afternoon.*

Right: *A short walk through Penniless Porch leads to the Market Square. Surrounded by elegant shops, it is still the site of the weekly market.*

Opposite: *The Bishop's Palace is enclosed inside high walls and a moat. This is home to a selection of ducks and the famous swans trained to ring a bell at feeding time.*

Right: *Vicars' Close still houses the clergy of the Cathedral, and dates from the middle of the fourteenth century. It is the oldest street in Europe.*

The intricate stonework of the cloisters is seen to good effect with a low sun.

On the opposite side to the cloisters is the fourteenth-century Cathedral clock that chimes animatedly on the hour.

Dulverton is a wonderful Exmoor town. The offices of the National Park Authority are here in this former workhouse, watched over by the statue of Lorna Doone.

The village of Washford was the home of Cleeve Abbey – a Cistertian monastery now in ruins and cared for by English Heritage. Visitors enter through a thirteenth-century gatehouse.

Dunster's Castle looks down on the High Street which is 'big' on tourism and lined with gift shops, craft shops, hotels and tearooms to help visitors spend their money.

At the top of the High Street is the six-sided Yarn Market, dating from 1609 when the village was an important cloth-manufacturing centre.

This is probably the most photographed cottage in Dunster, surrounded by a wonderful cottage garden. It is found on the way to the pack-horse bridge.

The intriguing Old Nunnery in Dunster has its upper floors and roof completely covered with slate.

Somerton's Market Cross of 1673 bears an uncanny similarity with the Yarn Market at Dunster. Somerton is the epitome of a rural Somerset market town.

Glastonbury's Market Cross is a little more streamlined than Somerton's.

A few yards away sits The Tribunal building whose sixteenth-century façade makes it stand out from the rest of the High Street architecture.

St Mary's church in Ilminster is a very grand affair with a central tower not dissimilar to that of Wells Cathedral.

Exford is in the heart of hunting country – mainly for the red deer that roam on Exmoor. Its village green is particularly attractive.

Above: *Selworthy is probably the prettiest village in Somerset — its cluster of thatched cottages nestle in a steep valley on Selworthy Beacon.*
The village is largely owned by the National Trust who were given it, along with the Holnicote Estate, by the Acland family.

Opposite: *Bow Cottage has a good example of the circular bread ovens that were attached to the chimneys of the cottages on the Holnicote Estate.*

Opposite: *Visitors driving through Cheddar Gorge often miss the intriguing silhouette of Lion Rock. Get the angle right and you'll see exactly how it got its name.*

Right: *Stawell is a delightful village in the Polden Hills and this colourful rural scene caught my eye on one particular visit – a mixture of new growth and old decay I suppose.*

*Above: The pack-horse bridge at Allerford is another favourite view of the calendar publishers.
The mottled-green tree canopy beyond gives this view a little extra interest.*

Opposite: Tall chimneys and thatched roofs are characteristic of cottages in this part of West Somerset. This delightful example is in Bossington.

Overleaf: The Polden Hills as seen from Burrow Mump. A shaft of sunlight spotlights the village of Middlezoy – 'zoy' being a Norse word for 'island'. These were areas of higher ground that stood proud of the flooded Levels that surrounded them – thus making an excellent site for a settlement.

Moorlynch church is a splendid example of a rural parish church. This one looks out from the Polden Hills over the Levels below. Note the three unmarked graves.

GRAND HOUSES
AND THEIR GARDENS

Somerset is particularly well blessed with grand houses. Not just houses, for in this chapter I have included the impressive Dunster Castle that dominates the village. The National Trust own several of the grand houses and have restored their fabric and their gardens in magnificent style. Montacute House and Barrington Court are worthy of mention for historical and architectural reasons alone, but their gardens are truly resplendent. There are also those properties where the gardens are of greater interest than the houses they belong to; Tintinhull House and Hestercombe House for example. One of the gardens featured here doesn't even belong to a house – it is the garden of a factory and contains an original railway viaduct!

Lytes Cary Manor is a comparatively modest National Trust property although it has an interesting history.
This fine example of topiary lines the path to the entrance door.

Surrounding the house are extensive gardens that are extremely tranquil. This view shows the
fourteenth-century chapel on the far right and impressive mullioned windows.

Barrington Court is a magnificent sixteenth-century manor house near Ilminster. To the left is Strode House – a later addition but now converted to a tearoom and luxury flats.

Barrington is surrounded by a number of individual garden 'rooms' with different themes. This is the stunning White Garden.

The Pool Garden has a central water feature surrounded by deep herbaceous borders, all of which are enclosed in a walled garden.

The Kitchen Garden is another walled garden that still provides a wide selection of fruit and vegetables for the house.
Notice how the beds are edged with colourful spring flowers.

This attractive wooden bridge crosses a small moat feature and gives access to the main gardens at Barrington.

Montacute is the grandest of Somerset's grand houses. From the west it is approached along a long drive. It is now in the care of the National Trust.

The lawns and borders to the east of the house are absolutely magnificent and are notable for the unusual shape of the gazebos in the corners.

Outside the present tearoom is a peaceful courtyard, complete with hand pump and colourful containers. The house is built from a local stone known as Ham stone.

Looking down on the courtyard from one of Montacute's gable-ends is this strange creature of indeterminate species!

The gardens at Tintinhull House are of far more interest than the house. These are the colourful borders of Eagle Court – one of whom can be seen on the pillar.

The deep borders of the Pool Garden are at their best in the summer.

Another view of the Pool Garden with its well-filled containers surrounding the actual pool.

The Mulberry Garden used
to be called the Showerings
Garden and was attached to
the factory that turned Somerset
pears into 'Babycham' in
Shepton Mallet. Sadly, it
is not open to the public.
The viaduct used to carry the
Somerset & Dorset Railway
over the garden.

Once open to the public but now a private house, Brympton d'Evercy is an imposing mansion with its own chapel and lake. This is the seventeenth-century south front.

The oldest part of the house dates from about 1520 and is on the north side. The chapel is over on the right and in the centre is a rather imposing dovecot.

Dunster Castle dominates the village from its imposing site. When it was first built the Bristol Channel used to lap against the rock on which it stands.

It has all the usual 'castle' architecture – turrets, towers and castellations – including this fortified gatehouse.

Its gardens are built on ledges and terraces that surround the castle – like the Keep Garden which was actually built on top of a huge water tank used to supply the rest of the village.

Hadspen House Gardens have been transformed by its present occupiers. The unusual curved walls shelter colourful borders with co-ordinated colour planting and a vegetable garden.

Within the gardens are a row of slate-roofed cottages with an interesting ridge line.

Hestercombe House Gardens above Taunton surround the
headquarters of the Somerset Fire Service. This view
shows The Plat, designed by Sir Edwin Lutyens
and planted by Gertrude Jekyll.

Opposite: *Another view of The Plat with its colourful planting.*

Above: *The terraces below the house contain interesting features such as this semi-circular pool
and plants like white and red valerian growing out of the terrace walls themselves.*

Behind the National Trust's Clevedon Court is an unusual garden that is both walled and terraced. The borders face south and are full of summer colour.

CURIOSITIES

This is the chapter where I've put all the pictures that don't immediately fall into one of the others. It is a real mixture of all the quirky, unusual or interesting bits of Somerset that are worthy of inclusion in this book. There are views of the natural landscape, memorials, buildings, ruins and shipwrecks – all of which have an interesting appearance, history or story behind them.

Left: *Not the real 'Excalibur' but a lifelike replica of the 'sword in the stone' on display outside the Somerset County Museum in Taunton Castle.*

Opposite: *If there's one landmark that says 'Somerset' it is this – Glastonbury Tor with its fifteenth-century tower of St Michael on the summit.*

With uncanny similarities to Glastonbury Tor, Burrow Mump also has a ruined church
on its summit, although this one dates from about 1793.

The Mump was donated to the National Trust
as a permanent monument from the county of Somerset
to those who fell during the Second World War.

This is all that remains of the SS Nornan, *driven ashore by a south-westerly gale during March 1897.*
It is now a tourist attraction known as the 'Berrow Wreck'.

This monument was erected in 1801 and marks the site of Athelney Abbey.
Founded by King Alfred in 877, it was allegedly the site where he 'burnt the cakes'.

The Battle of Sedgemoor in 1685 finally ended the Duke of Monmouth's claim to the English throne. This memorial in a field near Westonzoyland on the Levels marks the site of the last battle on English soil.

Somerset's oldest bridge crosses Exmoor's River Barle at Tarr Steps. It is a 180-feet-long – possibly prehistoric – clapper bridge and is constructed from huge stone slabs raised on stone pillars.

The ruins of Glastonbury's once magnificent Abbey contains a site discovered by the monks in 1191 which they claimed to be King Arthur's tomb.

The only complete building in the entire Abbey ruins site is the Abbot's Kitchen where four ovens were kept busy feeding the considerable number of inhabitants.

Above: This unique 1779 lock-up is where Castle Cary's criminals cooled their heels. It was only 7ft in diameter and must have been quite cramped with more than about three felons!

Opposite: England's last thatched windmill is Stembridge Tower Mill at High Ham and is a popular subject for artists. It is now the property of the National Trust.

Whitewashed churches are rare in Somerset. This unusual example is at Selworthy and enjoys stunning views across Exmoor from its churchyard.

AGRICULTURE

Somerset's mild, moist climate has promoted a rich diversity of agriculture throughout the county. The dairy cows that graze the lush pastures on the Levels and slopes of the lower hills have produced an industry that created the world famous Cheddar cheese. The area around Cheddar, on the warm southern slopes of the Mendips, is also the centre of an extensive strawberry-growing area. It is sufficiently warm in Somerset for crops once unheard of to be grown. Sunflowers, grapes and linseed are now quite common as well as the more widespread oil-seed rape. There are, of course, farms that grow non-food crops such as daffodils and the uniquely Somerset crop of withies. These are varieties of willow that are harvested from the Levels, boiled, stripped of their bark and exported across the world to be turned into basketware. Finally, we musn't forget the one crop that more people associate with Somerset than any other – the cider apples that ferment into a real liquid asset for the county.

The blossom on these apple trees overlooking the Levels will soon fall to leave behind what is perhaps Somerset's greatest crop – cider apples.

Ray Stanlake – cider maker.

This could almost be a scene shot in Tuscany – but it is not. This is Lytes Cary near Somerton and the bright yellow crop in the field is sunflowers.

Somerset's climate is also warm enough for the cultivation of vines. These Faber grapes are at Moorlynch Vineyard on the Polden Hills.

Spring arrives early in Somerset and daffodil bulbs like growing in the moist peaty soil of the Levels – like here on Butleigh Moor.

Withies are the raw material for the basketware industry –
harvested from the fields on the Levels, boiled until black
and then stripped of their bark to reveal the orange tint so
characteristic of 'baskets' the world over. Growing them
is the easy bit – it is the skill of the basket weaver
that produces the finished product.

Overleaf: The end of the harvest in a field
near Kingsdon – and the end of this book.